AquaGuide

Lake Tanganyika Cichlids

Frank Schneidewind

CONTENTS

Originally published in Germany in 1997 by bede-Verlag, Bühlfelderweg 12, D-94239 Ruhmannsfelden

© 1997 by bede-Verlag

First published in the UK in 2002 by Interpet Publishing, Vincent Lane, Dorking, Surrey RH4 3YX, UK

English text © 2002 by Interpet Publishing Ltd.

ISBN 1-84286-036-4

The recommendations in this book are given without any guarantees on the part of the author and publisher. If in doubt, seek the advice of a vet or aquatic specialist.

Translation: Stephen Hunter

Unless otherwise credited, all photographs in this book are from Frank Schneidewind. The author thanks "Aqua-Treff Berlin", especially Mr Sascha Wendland, for allowing him to take photographs.

The cichlids of Lake Tanganyika are in many respects unique fish, and they have long enjoyed great popularity among aquarists. Even within the fascinating cichlid family they enjoy special status, and there is probably no other aspect of the world of aquariums that has spawned so much specialization. For example, there are enthusiasts who concentrate solely on the so-called sand cichlids, featherfins, shell dwellers, sardine cichlids or perhaps on the hugely varied *Tropheus* genus. Among these specialists a healthy exchange of thoughts, ideas and, most important of all, of breeding fish has grown up. As a consequence of this development, which has proved to be more than just a passing fad, various ornamental fish catchers and exporters have set up residence on the shores of the lake and sell the much sought-after cichlids (some of them wild-caught, others bred on fish farms) to enthusiasts all round the world, whose craving for new varieties seems boundless. Not all Lake Tanganyika cichlids can be described as economical to buy, and for a variety of reasons many of the species are among the most expensive of all freshwater fish. Furthermore, not all Lake Tanganyika cichlids are suitable for beginners.

Lake Tanganyika cichlids are not only popular among aquarists: their highly-developed social behaviour and great regional diversity make them ideal subjects for behavioural researchers, evolutionary biologists and geneticists. Part of the reason that so many aquarists

keep Lake Tanganyika cichlids can be explained objectively, while another part rests in the subjective pleasure and fascination to be gained from these extraordinary fish. Around 300 species of fish populate this African lake, and just under 200 of them are cichlids. Lake Tanganyika and its fish population break many records between them. For example, both the largest cichlid, the 80cm (31in) long *Boulengerochromis microlepsis* and one of the smallest, the 3.5cm (1.4in) long *Lamprologus*

Often it is the concealed life of many species that is most fascinating. Lake Tanganyika cichlids will intrigue you at every stage in their life cycle. Spathodus erythrodon.

Special cichlids

kungweensis, come from this lake in the heart of Africa.

Every year collecting expeditions organized by ambitious aquarists unearth new species, and many more will undoubtedly be added to the list, while much no doubt remains to be learned about their proper classification. Virtually all the lake's cichlids live only there and nowhere else in the world (a phenomenon known as endemism), and almost all possible methods of reproduction are prevalent among them. By contrast, in neighbouring Lake Malawi mouthbrooders predominate. In Lake Tanganyika everything is far more complicated, and correspondingly more interesting. With its vast size, this rift lake is in fact a major inland sea, and at 1470m (4823ft) in depth, it is the second deepest lake in the world after Lake Baikal in Siberia. Geologists

estimate that it is over ten million years old, and for most of this period it was totally isolated. This means it is significantly older than either Lake Malawi or Lake Victoria.

Over this immense stretch of time a huge variety of species has developed. Evolution has simply had much more time to do its work and allow cichlid species to adapt to local conditions. This

down catfish. The striking-looking cuckoo synodontis (e.g. *Synodontis multipunctatus*) take the cichlid's eggs during spawning into their mouths and intermingle them with their own offspring. The earlier-hatching catfish fry then feed on the cichlid young in the host's mouth. Brood parasitism among fish, who would have thought it!

The principal fascination of Lake

The fearsome mouth and general appearance of this species is reminiscent of the black tiger fish. Altolamprologus compressiceps "Goldhead".

has led to the great number of cichlid genera, the largest in Africa. A variety of other fish species have developed alongside the cichlids, leading to remarkable phenomena such as the parasitism on cichlid broods by upside-

Tanganyika cichlids lies in their diversity of body shapes and their fascinating behaviour. For example, there are fish which have been given appropriate nicknames, such as sardine cichlids (the *Cyprichomis* and *Paracyprichromis*

genera) or goby cichlids (*Eretmodini*). These popular names reflect noteworthy morphological similarities in linguistically logical ways. Since bodily structures everywhere adapt to the environment, comparable conditions in different locations will lead to physical similarities, and these can be very confusing for non-specialists. Of course, many of the species have attractive external colouring, but the chief fascination in keeping them lies in their varied and easy-to-observe behavioural patterns. Lake Tanganyika cichlids are among the most aggressive of freshwater fish. This means that some of them require very specific individual treatment in the aquarium and sensitive handling,

which adds to the fascination and challenge involved in keeping them. Examples are available on the market to suit every budget, taste and aquarium, and many cave spawners can be kept and bred in tanks as small as 50 litres (11gal) in capacity.

Naturally the best proof of the correct application of the knowledge and experience you have built up comes when you successfully breed from your fish, the most satisfying moment in the life of every aquarist. Nobody can lay down a precise formula for breeding success, and this is nowhere truer than with Lake Tanganyika cichlids.

Nevertheless, I hope that this slim volume will provide useful advice for

Tropheus species are sensitive creatures requiring special treatment. Tropheus sp. llangi.

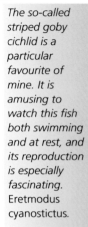

The so-called striped goby cichlid is a particular favourite of mine. It is amusing to watch this fish both swimming and at rest, and its reproduction is especially fascinating. Eretmodus cyanostictus.

those embarking on the adventure of keeping Lake Tanganyika cichlids. For reasons of space I will not be able to go into every last detail, rather I will endeavour to offer tips enabling you to make a good start with the fascinating hobby of keeping and breeding Lake Tanganyika cichlids.

One initial point: as you will appreciate, the key to the successful breeding of Lake Tanganyika cichlids lies in an exact understanding of their environmental conditions and the resultant peculiarities in their behaviour and care requirements. You are holding the key in your two hands!

The many facets of reproduction

The most fascinating aspect of the social interaction of Lake Tanganyika cichlids is their hugely-varied reproductive behaviour. All cichlids brood their young, and Lake Tanganyika species are no exception. The most basic form of reproduction among cichlids is substrate spawning. Substrate-spawning species seek out an unprotected spot suitable for laying eggs, and this is then vigorously defended by the parents. Even simpler methods are found among other fish species, which simply squirt eggs and sperm into the water in an uncontrolled manner, but this method of spawning onto an unprotected substrate is the most primitive method

of reproduction found among the cichlids, and the most hazardous for their young. The adults do look after the eggs and fry, but the degree of care is hardly optimal. The resulting spawn

is normally copious in quantity. The strategy of substrate spawners can be summed up like this: they produce a large quantity of fertilized eggs at great expense in order to ensure that a few survive at the end of the day. In Lake Tanganyika there are few true substrate spawners. *Boulangererochromis microlepis*, cited in the previous chapter as the largest of all cichlids, is the best-known of the Lake Tanganyika substrate spawners.

The logical next evolutionary step, offering a variety of advantages and changes, is to spawn in a concealed location. Depositing the spawn in a cave or other secure location is clearly a more elegant strategy. The hidden spawn is concealed from predators, but is energetically defended nevertheless. The cave spawning of the generally popular species of the *Julidochromis* and (*Neo-*) *Lamprologus* genera is particularly exciting and easy to observe. These species can be recommended to beginners, who will find them captivating, particularly when they start breeding. *Julidochromis* species, for example, lay their generally green-coloured eggs overhead on the top of the cave, a phenomenon seldom observed by the aquarist, who often does not realize that spawning has taken place until the young fry emerge. As events unfold the observer will be fascinated to discover further fry emerging, and to see that the older offspring participate in the protection of their younger siblings by defending the spawning area

Mouthbrooding is the most advanced form of brood care. The spawning process is very similar in the majority of mouthbrooders. This series of pictures illustrates how the process unfolds. Tropheus *sp.* "Kachese Red".

1

5

2

3 & 4

Reproduction

Right:
Eretmodus
cyanostictus.

*Far right: In
almost all goby
cichlids, the
males and
females share
the task of
mouth-
brooding. After
about ten days
the female
transfers the
brood to the
male.*
Tanganicodus
irsacae.

and in some species even assisting their parents in looking after the spawn. This apparently unselfish co-operation is unique among fish and is known as altruism. This behaviour has contributed to the fame of the best-known of all Lake Tanganyika cichlids, the fairy cichlid, *Neolamprologus brichardi*. A further large group of small Lake Tanganyika cichlids (among them the well-known *Lamprologus ocellatus*) favours an even more unusual reproductive strategy, namely spawning in empty snail shells!

The development of cave spawning does have the "unromantic" side effect that, whereas genuine substrate spawning involves the two parents sticking together at all times, the long-term concealment of the spawn inevitably leads to a division of labour. One partner, normally the female, looks after the spawn while the male guards the area against intruders.

Thus their bond is weakened and their separate specializations lead to the development of distinct physical characteristics. This means that potential reproductive partners can be identified more swiftly and the preliminary courtship displays become briefer. From a reproductive point of view it is more efficient for the male to be able to distribute his comparatively minor investment, the sperm, among several females, the resultant social structure being known as a harem. However, evolution has taken one further extraordinary step. While the spawn was already well-protected on the roof of a cave, cichlid evolution has come up with the most elegant solution of all: mouthbrooding. There could hardly be a more secure location than in the body of the parent itself, and where better than the mouth? This specialization represents a virtually perfect evolutionary adaptation.

10

Mouthbrooding fish look after their offspring long after they hatch, only releasing them in a safe spot after the fry have exhausted their supplies of yolk. At any sign of disturbance the fry return to the safety of the mother's throat sac. Some females even feed during the mouthbrooding period, and many fry start feeding on edible particles that drift into their mother's mouth. In some mouthbrooders of the *Cyprochromis* genus, the skin of the throat pouch is transparent, allowing the teeming fry inside to view the outside world, probably enabling them to gather experience from a secure vantage point.

The major evolutionary step to mouthbrooding is easier to understand when we remember that a degree of care involving the mouth already takes place in the case of substrate spawners, which use their mouths to sort out eggs, transport spawn and corral straying fry. The female's throat pouch is naturally limited in size, and accordingly the quantity of eggs produced is drastically reduced. However, this means in turn that the fish can afford to produce larger eggs, and a larger egg means a larger store of yolk, giving the embryos a major advantage, enabling them to feed off larger objects at an earlier age, making

Lake Tanganyika cichlids show such highly diverse behaviour, and not only in their reproductive methods, that aquarists are bound to be in for some surprises. Enantiopus melanogenys.

Reproduction

The dummy egg spots on the anal fin are seldom very pronounced among Lake Tanganyika cichlids. Astatoreo-chromis cf. vanderhorsti.

Among the well-known featherfins the egg spots are at the ends of their prolonged ventral fins. Opthalmo-tilapia nasuta.

them more robust. Thus while the amount of spawn produced gets smaller and smaller, the eggs get bigger and bigger, and the hatched fry correspondingly stronger. With this method of brooding it is not so vital for both parents to defend the spawn. From the point of view of reproductive success it is more efficient for the female alone to watch over the spawn while the male is able to devote himself to further procreation with other female fish. This in turn means the end of monogamy and consequently the end of any male-female bond lasting beyond the procreative act itself.

Among our Lake Tanganyika cichlids many examples can be found that employ this evolutionary development, or that embody various intermediate stages in this transitional process. Particularly interesting in this context are the ever-popular goby cichlids, where several different transitional stages can be found within a closely related group of species. For example, in the well-known striped goby cichlid, *Eretmodus cyanostictus*, brooding is shared by both parents, with the spawn being transferred from the female to the male about halfway through the incubation period.

The evolutionary process leading to mouthbrooding has thrown up some extraordinary phenomena. For example, in order to ensure that the eggs are fertilized during the extremely brief reproductive act, many Lake Tanganyika cichlids bear dummy egg spots on their anal fins. Their original purpose was to divert the female's attention to these sham eggs during spawning in order to ensure that the male's sperm is directed accurately into the female's mouth.

The reason for this is that the female fish thinks that the "eggs" must be gathered up, and instinctively snaps at the spread anal fins, and thus in the

Reproduction

New species and unknown colour variants of old favourites are continually being discovered in our aquariums. Neolamprologus marunguensis.

direction of the genital papillae. This phenomenon is known to biologists as mimicry or auto-mimicry. However, these dummy egg spots are seldom as prominent on Lake Tanganyika cichlids as they are on many Lake Malawi cichlids, which are renowned for them.

On the other hand, only in Lake Tanganyika are species found (of the genus *Ophthalmotilapia*) where the egg spots are located elegantly on the end of a prolonged ventral fin. The final preliminary step in the direction of the ideal brood method has been taken by the well-known *Cyprichromis leptosoma*. To shorten the hazardous spawning process and make it independent of a substrate, reproductive methods have evolved in which some cichlids, such as *Cyprichromis leptosoma*, simply spawn in open water.

It is remarkable how many times mouthbrooding has evolved independently in different parts of the world, and fascinating to see how many different reproductive methods exist among our Lake Tanganyika cichlids. Such diversity is found nowhere else in the world, making the lake a uniquely valuable locale for the study of the evolution of brooding techniques via living species and "behavioural fossils". The high proportion of cave-spawning cichlid species in Lake Tanganyika, in marked contrast to Lake Malawi, is probably due to the different history of Lake Tanganyika and to its earlier connection to the Zaire drainage basin, where substrate spawners predominate. Furthermore, cave spawners find an ideal environment among the boulder-strewn shores of Lake Tanganyika, and it appears that as a consequence the selective evolutionary pressure in the direction of mouthbrooding is not as great here as it is in neighbouring Lake Malawi.

The wide variety of brooding methods has been discovered first and foremost by aquarists, whose accumulated knowledge and experience will be indispensable to help you to look after and breed your own fish satisfactorily. However, many species have never been successfully bred in captivity, and others only sporadically so or by accident. Many secrets and puzzles remain to be solved, and as an inquisitive aquarist with your own aquarium you will have the opportunity to delve into them and explore at your leisure.

Welcome to the voyage of discovery!

Although the demands posed by Lake Tanganyika cichlids are many and varied, there are a number of useful general guidelines for newcomers, as well as some handy tips for finding your way through the jungle of aquarium products on the market. Once you have decided on the fish you wish to keep and chosen a tank of appropriate size, you will have to select a suitable location for your aquarium. Most beginners opt for an all-in-one combination unit consisting of an aquarium stand, a suitable hood and the glass tank itself. These all-in-one units are available in a variety of colours and wood finishes and provide a simple and straightforward way of getting

started without having to tangle with any DIY.

Before paying for your tank, however, you should consider where you are going to put it. Unsuitable home locations include window areas and positions near heaters or doors. You should also take into account the load on the floor resulting from the aquarium gravel plus the weight of the filled tank itself. You will have to give the strength of your floor serious consideration if your aquarium is going to weigh more than a ton. Additionally, the floor surface must be completely flat. If in any doubt, consult a structural engineer. It is in any case advisable, to be on the safe side,

Porous rock is a highly decorative aquarium material which contrasts well with the plants and the blue background.

The aquarium

Suitably decorated, a Lake Tanganyika aquarium can provide an attractive centrepiece for your living room

Despite all the technology and attractive decor in your tank, the fish should always remain the true focus of attention.

Lake Tanganyika cichlids make up for their lack of colour by their extraordinary variety of shapes and lifestyles. Here, for example, we see a group of shell-dwellers.

to take out adequate household contents insurance. There is no need for excessive concern, though, for aquariums have long since ceased to be the ticking timebombs they once were. Thanks to the excellent properties of silicone sealants, strong, high-grade glass can now be used to construct robust tanks ensuring the safety of the creatures now dependent on you for their well-being. Glass aquariums sealed with black silicone have the best reputation.

After your basic decision regarding your chosen fish and a suitable aquarium based on the space available at home and the needs of the fish you intend to keep, you should give careful attention to the "internals" of the aquarium. We will start by considering an item that is vital for every aquarium and will prolong its life: a layer of cushioning material between the underside of the tank and the surface on which it sits. This may be a piece of old carpet, expanded polystyrene or the soft matting which is widely available commercially. Any of these materials will provide a buffer zone preventing localized stress-points in the glass bottom due to small pieces of grit, etc., which can eventually lead to cracking.

Now you can turn your thoughts to the business of aquarium design. Firstly

The aquarium

there is the question of choosing a suitable background which will not only be attractive for human viewers but also appropriate for the occupants of the tank. This is largely a matter of taste, but do bear in mind that some options are difficult to remove once put in place, and that you will have to put up with the sight of them for years. Unfortunately in my view, the simplest and most common solution is the unimaginative option of sticking on some kind of multicoloured poster background, but each to his own I suppose. An attractive addition to an otherwise monotonous selection of posters is the new range of Japanese photographic backgrounds featuring some spectacular rocky seascapes. Another striking option is to use one

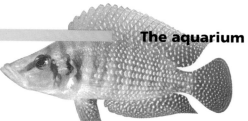

of the single-colour films available, which can be stuck onto the back wall of the tank, offering a practical and economical solution. In my experience blue tones give the most natural and strongly contrasting background, conveying an impression of greater depth. Some resourceful aquarists construct their own so-called dry dioramas behind the aquarium, giving the impression of added size to their underwater aquascapes.

Many options also exist for the inside of the aquarium. In this connection, polystyrene is easy to work and shape. Ready-made backgrounds are commercially available, either for placing behind the aquarium or sticking to the inside of the back wall. A wide range of relief backgrounds and ceramic items are also available. Make an appropriate selection from the variety on offer, bearing in mind not just your own tastes but also the needs of the future inhabitants of the tank.

After selecting your background, you can turn your attention to the substrate. Much could be written here without exhausting the whole subject. The variety of materials on the market ranges from glass marbles to rocks the size of a child's head. The colour of the substrate is more than just a matter of taste, rather being a question of optical effect. Standard light sand-coloured quartz gravel can generally be recommended. One area where many make a mistake is in the amount of gravel needed, with inadequate

quantities often being recommended. The substrate not only provides a bed for the plants you place in the aquarium, it also represents a vast breeding ground for bacteria, a matter we shall be discussing further later. Both over-coarse gravel and very fine sand are unsuitable for aquariums. Excessively large grain sizes allow particles of food to slip between the gaps and putrefy, while with a very fine grain size insufficient water will be able to flow through the substrate and around the plant roots growing in it, meaning that the gravel eventually goes foul. You will not go far wrong with grain sizes between one and three millimetres.

Matters are different as regards the correct lighting. All-in-one aquariums come with fitted hoods with inbuilt splashproof lighting fixtures which as a rule are only designed to take two light elements. Of course you can increase the number of lights you use provided the hood has space for them, and most aquarists have to be satisfied with this. In the case of Lake Tanganyika cichlids, I recommend providing the tank with plenty of strong lighting from above as this displays these marvellous fish, most of them accustomed to bright conditions in their natural habitat, to best effect. If your aquarium hood has two fluorescent lamp sockets, I recommend having one "Daylight" triphosphor tube and one "Beauty Light" tube. The white daylight tube provides very bright, slightly blue-tinged light, while the Beauty Light, a so-called "plant lamp", emits a pleasing

The illustration shows a 200-litre (44gal) breeding tank containing the fry of several different Lake Tanganyika cichlids. Red artificial stones, a commercially available background and some anubias provide the decoration.

violet light. In my experience the combination of these two different kinds of light gives a very attractive optical effect. The Beauty Light supplies that touch of sunshine lacking in the cold white of the daylight tube. It is better to place the Beauty Light tube in the front socket rather than in the rear one, where its light will be washed out by the daylight tube, so that the desired blend of colours is not achieved. And of course it is this which also allows the plants to grow. A useful item of equipment is a time switch to regulate automatically the desired illumination periods of 12 to 14 hours. Related to the question of lighting is that of a top cover. With modern sealed aquarium hoods the justification for the top glass cover disappears. Condensed water that forms on the hood drips back into the tank, and suicidal fish simply bounce off the hard plastic surface and back into the water.

Once this important point has also been dealt with, you can address the various other issues of aquarium technology. Firstly, there is heating. All aquariums need heating at least some of the time, for water temperatures continually in excess of 25°C (77°F) cannot be achieved simply from the ambient heat of your home. Accordingly you will need at least one aquarium heater. Refer to the guides produced by heater manufacturers to choose suitable units for your tank. It is advisable to employ heaters with built-in thermostats to ensure that a constant temperature is maintained. These are usually standard equipment nowadays. These units are also fitted with a dry-running failsafe device, but should nevertheless be unplugged whenever you do anything inside the aquarium.

Less straightforward is the choice of a suitable filter, at first sight at any rate. The size of your aquarium is obviously a major factor here. In my experience of various different set-ups, internal filters work well in tanks up to 80cm (30in) long, while any longer or larger capacity tank (> 100 litres/22gal) will require an

to the inside of the tank with the aid of simple rubber suckers, ideally with the outlet facing upwards to facilitate the water flow.

External filters are a somewhat more complex matter, showing significant variations in price which do not always reflect the actual quality or efficiency of the models involved. They generally consist of a plastic container (the canister) with the motor sitting on top housed in the lid. Thus the filter is completely external to the aquarium and is connected to it by unsightly but, unfortunately, unavoidable hoses. They are not always entirely straightforward to install and maintain. You must allow more time for cleaning the aquarium as a whole. For these few (five to ten) times in the year you should avail yourself of a fast coupling system, an extremely handy accessory device which makes the work of separating the filter from the aquarium significantly easier.

The secret of the success of external filters lies in the filtration media used. With this kind of filter the aquarium water is not filtered through a single cartridge but through several different filtering materials. Ask to see the filter media which go with your preferred model of filter. One important tip is that you do not have to use activated carbon on a continual basis, while quantities of fine filter wool are not advisable generally, as they soon lead to blockages. The efficacy of the filter will of course depend on the size of your aquarium. These days the many

external filter of some kind in order to function well. In both cases the filters will incorporate motor-driven pumps of which a great variety of different models are available. Electric internal filters use foam-filled cartridges to trap particles suspended in the water and provide efficient basic mechanical filtering. As a rule they have to be cleaned once a week by rinsing out the filter sponge. All in all this represents an extremely simple and practical system, and their installation generally involves simply attaching them

Among cichlid fanciers the most popular plant types are from the Anubias genus.

suppliers of filters have learned that the performance of a filter can suffer as a result of kinks in the hose, dirty filtering material, etc. The water in your aquarium should cycle through the filter two to three times per hour if it is to be entirely effective.

With Lake Tanganyika cichlids it is particularly important also to use an aeration pump. The simplest system consists of an airpump, a length of hose and the airstone of your choice. All of these devices do, unfortunately, make a certain amount of noise which takes some getting used to (professional aquarists wake up at night when the noise stops!), though it can be muffled to a certain extent by an underlay of foam or other suitable material. The pump must always be situated outside the aquarium and if possible located above water level. If this is not possible, then it is advisable to fit a check valve to prevent water running back into the pump in the event of a power cut.

Only now can we get started on what most aquarists view as the real business:

the tank decoration. More superb decorative materials are now commercially available for different kinds of aquarium than you can possibly imagine. Always bear in mind the weight to which the glass tank will be subjected. If you are using heavy rocks, a sheet of expanded polystyrene, either glued to the bottom glass with silicone sealant or placed under particularly heavy items, will provide protection. The extremely high buoyancy of polystyrene makes the former option preferable. The tank furnishings are particularly important in the case of Lake Tanganyika cichlids, given their liking for concealment. Clay and ceramic caves, upturned flowerpots with entry holes, coconut shells or even piled-up plates, pipes, bricks, etc. will provide the necessary shelter for harassed fish, and also serve as brood caves or spawning grounds for many cichlid pairs and as boundary markers for their territories. Take every opportunity to look at other aquarists' tanks, and also at aquariums at exhibitions and aquatic centres, in order to seek inspiration for your own tank's decoration. What to use is not a problem, with a profusion of different coloured slates, stones and porous rock being among the most popular materials available. Roots, however tempting their attractive shapes may make them, are inadvisable since they will increase the acidity of the water.

Do not overcrowd your tank with fish or you will not leave sufficient space for plants. When stocking your aquarium with plants think in terms of foreground, middle ground and background. You will quickly appreciate how important depth is to your decorations, which will truly come into their own at a depth of 40cm (16in) or greater. Different types of plant are suited to each of your three tank areas. These will not always be native African plants, but this should not concern you.

My own aquarium is stocked in the foreground with cryptocoryne, in the middle ground with larger swordplants (*Echinodorus*) and water ferns (*Ceratopteris*) in the background. I use a lot of porous rock, and on it I plant African anubias, Java ferns (*Microsorium*) and African water fern (*Bolbitis*). This selection is sparing not only because these are favourite plants of mine, but also because many Lake Tanganyika cichlids are tough on plants, shredding them or even digging them up. Many fish which hide their spawn, however, will thrive in "botanical aquariums", and plants are not simply pleasing to the eye – a good selection of them is a must for every healthy, properly functioning aquarium.

CHECKLIST

✓ You want to start an aquarium and will need a suitable tank to do so.

✓ You are aware of your responsibility for all future inhabitants of the aquarium and are looking forward to observing its fascinating occupants.

✓ You have made the right choice and have decided to keep Lake Tanganyika cichlids (using this book as a reference).

✓ Your local tap water is suitable (> 10°dGH, > pH 7).

✓ Take care to select a suitable location in your home. It does not have to be earthquake-proof but it must be strong enough to support an aquarium.

✓ Select an aquarium complete with a purpose-built stand suitable for the space you have available, your requirements and your pocket.

✓ Carefully check your tank for leaks and glass fractures before filling it.

✓ Now put in your preferred background.

✓ Thoroughly rinse the fine-grain substrate you are using and put it into the aquarium, after first inserting a polystyrene sheet to protect the bottom if necessary, using aquarium silicone sealant to bond it to the glass.

✓ Choose suitably coloured overhead lighting for the aquarium.

✓ Choose a good-quality thermostatically controlled heater to heat the aquarium.

✓ Ensure clear, pure water by installing a suitable filter for the size of aquarium.

✓ To ensure your fish stay in good condition you should install an airstone powered by an airpump.

✓ Now get to work on the decorative aspect, setting up an underwater landscape providing the fish with plenty of shelter.

✓ Next add plants to create an underwater garden.

✓ Now read the following chapter to find out what you will need to do in order to look after your fish.

It is now important to follow a specific sequence of events in order to get your aquarium ready as quickly as possible and to ensure its long-term future. For both budding and experienced aquarists there is no sadder sight than an empty aquarium. However, you must curb your impatience a little longer! After you have got all the hardware and technology in place, you should now bone up on the instructions for installation in your aquarium. The sequence of events should be as follows:

If you have done everything correctly, your aquarium should now be bubbling and fizzing. Check that all decorative items and plants are firmly in place and, if necessary, drain off a little water if there is significant clouding.

There can be few hobbies which involve more accessory equipment, ranging from the indispensable to the pointless, than keeping an aquarium. We shall look at some of the more important modern aids to assist you in keeping a well-ordered aquarium.

✓ Thoroughly rinse your aquarium substrate in a bucket and spread it on the base of the tank, slightly increasing its depth from about 4cm (1.5in) at the front to 7cm (2.75in) at the back.

✓ Place washed decorative items in the tank.

✓ Place plants, minus any lead ties and plastic pots, into the gravel, first trimming the roots.

✓ Half-fill the tank with tap water brought to the right temperature, preferably by hose or using a bucket. To avoid excessive turbulence, place a plate or newspaper beneath the stream of water.

✓ Now rinse your filter medium or foam cartridge in running water and then connect your filter system.

✓ Attach the airpump to the air hose and airstone and place the stone in a suitable position where surface turbulence will not cause any problem.

✓ The thermostatically controlled heater should be placed towards the rear of the tank in an area with plenty of water circulation. Set the thermostat to 27°C (81°F).

✓ Check that all the technical equipment is working properly and turn all equipment that can be regulated to its highest setting.

✓ Now finish filling the aquarium with water.

It is advisable, not only when starting up but at every water change, to add a liquid water conditioner to neutralize the chlorine and heavy metals in the water, both of which can be toxic to fish. The conditioner will provide the fish with an effective and reliable scale protector. Also very useful, indeed virtually indispensable nowadays, is the use of a so-called "bio-starter". This highly beneficial fluid gives the sterile aquarium water an injection of all-important bacteria from day one. To appreciate the significance of this, one must understand how vital bacteria are to the complex ecosystem that develops in an aquarium. Their role is to dispose of all the waste matter in the aquarium (faeces, food particles, plant material, etc.) as quickly and non-toxically as possible. Without these bacteria, the whole ecosystem becomes imbalanced and the aquarium as a whole can come to grief.

The problem when starting up is that, while waste matter will be produced immediately, colonies of bacteria need time to establish themselves in the gravel and in the filter media. The plants in particular will benefit greatly if you initially invest in a few fertilizer tablets or laterite balls, which should be pressed into the gravel near plant roots. It is also advisable to add some liquid iron fertilizer regularly to the water to keep greenery healthy. It is possible that algae will initially gain the upper hand in your aquarium. However, this only represents a transitional phase during which the aquarium is sometimes said to be "running in". How long this phase lasts largely depends on

Algae are always an indication of an imbalance in the aquarium ecosystem. It is important to know the underlying cause rather than simply treating the symptoms.

your own skills, but you must be patient. Do not immediately take the radical step of using algae killers. Algae in any shape, form or colour are only a symptom of some kind of imbalance in the aquarium ecosystem. You should not concern yourself if a gentle green colour develops, and an ugly brown coloration may also have to be accepted during the initial stages. However, thread- or brushlike cultures of algae must be avoided. The question of algae is not, though, as complicated as it may at first appear. If you follow the guidelines laid down in this book, you should be spared any serious problems.

Once everything is in place, it is still not quite time to introduce your cichlid population to the aquarium. A tried-and-tested preliminary step is first to introduce some algae-eating catfish (*Ancistrus*). Over the following days your patience will be put to the test. You should wait one week, and if all the equipment is functioning correctly, then you can get started. However, before we turn to the questions of what fish to stock and fish compatibility, there are a number of other routine chores to take care of, the daily bread of a Lake Tanganyika aquarist as it were.

Looking after your cichlids

As might be expected, the care required by Lake Tanganyika cichlids is determined by the conditions in their natural habitat. This is seldom so essential as in this case: Lake Tanganyika is an extremely clear, pure, oxygen-rich body of water with highly unusual chemical properties. It is strongly alkaline, with a pH of up to 9, and is of medium to high hardness, measured in terms of both carbonate hardness and total hardness. Even at depth the water temperature is always above 20°C (68°F). The water contains an abundance of dissolved minerals and copious dissolved oxygen, and chemical pollution from nitrates is virtually non-existent. Lake Tanganyika cichlids, then, are used to very favourable conditions and are sensitive to water profiles differing from those of their natural habitat. Accordingly, if your local water conditions are not right (information about this can be obtained from your local water authority), you will unfortunately have to add chemicals to the water and filter it through crushed marble or coral. Do not overdo it, however! Lake Tanganyika cichlids cannot be kept without making these preparations, for these sensitive fish do not adapt to unfamiliar water conditions even after several generations.

Over the first few weeks, you must not neglect regular water changes. Even if you have filled your aquarium with fresh water and installed the fish only a few days previously, and everything still looks pure and clean, it is already time to change the water.

BASIC CARE

✓ No Lake Tanganyika cichlid can tolerate water temperatures over 30°C (86°F).

✓ All Lake Tanganyika cichlids are highly sensitive to acidic water, i.e. water with a pH value of less than 7.

✓ Lake Tanganyika cichlids will not thrive in old, stale water.

✓ Tanganyika cichlids are highly sensitive to shortage of oxygen.

The above points have the following consequences for aquarium maintenance:

✓ A weekly partial (50 per cent) water change is a must.

✓ Never allow the water temperature to rise above 30°C (86°F).

✓ Keep the airpump operating day and night.

✓ Do not overfeed your fish or overstock your tank.

✓ Regularly check the following chemical values: pH, total hardness, carbonate hardness and nitrate content, and take appropriate action if necessary.

In an aquarium, substances that you cannot see (for example nitrates) are often most dangerous. Moreover, every aquarium contains copious quantities of waste products (faeces, urine, food remains, etc.) right from the start. And, as we noted earlier, bacteria colonies will not have had time to establish themselves yet. Accordingly a water change is vital at this point, in order to remove chemical waste products and prevent the fish from being poisoned.

Another fundamental of caring for your cichlids is food. Cichlids generally have a reputation for being omnivores which will voraciously devour anything put their way from earthworms to breadcrumbs. However, when keeping Lake Tanganyika cichlids you will have to forget this, for although they will polish off more or less anything you throw into the tank, they will suffer the consequences later in the form of often-fatal indigestion and inflammatory conditions. Most Lake Tanganyika cichlids receive incorrect nourishment in the aquarium. The following five principal types of fish food should be selected:

Live food

Deep-frozen live food

Freeze-drived live food

Dried food in a variety of different forms (flakes, tablets, granules, pellets, etc.)

Home-reared fish food (e.g., enchytraea, white worms, brine shrimps)

These days many aquarists entirely avoid live food due to the unfortunate fact that disease transmission cannot be ruled out. The days when every true aquarist would go hunting for micro-organisms in ponds with a home-made fishing net, meeting other aquarists and enjoying the peace and tranquillity of the countryside, are now long gone. The modern city-dwelling aquarist would not know where to find these food sources, nor how to catch them, but he or she will no doubt know the location of a well-stocked deep freeze at a nearby aquatic centre or pet shop. I would recommend avoiding the commonly available mosquito larvae or *Tubifex* worms as they are often contaminated with toxins; instead use frozen food such as *Cyclops*, water fleas, *Artemia*, shrimps or special blends designed for Lake Tanganyika cichlids. If using flaked food, I recommend that you favour branded products and make sure you are aware of your fishes' feeding preferences. For example, suppliers offer special mixtures for herbivores, which include many Lake Tanganyika cichlids.

In recent years increasing numbers of granules, pellets and sticks have come onto the market, and sadly the satisfying but tedious practice of breeding one's own food has largely gone out of fashion, though some aquarists do still breed nauplii (larvae) from the eggs of brine shrimp (*Artemia salina*). This practice at least meant that you knew where the food you used had come from.

However, the range of commercially

Tropheus moorii are not only highly sensitive to their external conditions, they display a high degree of intraspecies aggression, and should be kept in large communities to minimize conflict.

available products is so extensive that there is no need to worry that your fish are in danger of starving or suffering from malnutrition, and it is important never to overfeed them. When feeding them, nothing should fall to the bed of the aquarium. Throwing in two to five small but varied pinches a day will ensure the well-being of your stock, and an occasional day of fasting will do them no harm.

Another advisable standard practice is to quarantine new stock in a separate tank to prevent the transmission of any diseases they may be harbouring to the existing stock. The tank you use for this purpose should be up to the same technical standards as your main aquarium, but does not have to be as large. New fish should be observed carefully for at least two weeks for any signs of a fish disease.

Lake Tanganyika cichlids are susceptible to any illness you may find in specialist books on tropical fish diseases, and I will limit myself here to a few of the most important conditions. Be on the look-out during the first few days for the formation of white spots (*Ichthyophthirius*) on the scales. Before this happens, the fish will generally indicate their discomfort by retracting their fins and shying away from objects in the aquarium. These spots are small parasites which proliferate with great speed and will

Tropheus moorii are virtually herbivores and must be fed with ballast-rich plant materials for their well-being. Tropheus sp. "Red Rainbow".

Sand cichlids sift through the fine aquarium substrate in search of food. Enantiopus melanogenys.

be fatal if not treated in time. However, a wide variety of effective preparations are commercially available, and to speed the recovery process it is a good idea to raise the water temperature to 30°C (86°F) for three days. If this does not get the white spots under control, then the ailment is velvet disease (*Oodinium*), which also presents with fine white spots. Counteracting this disease is a somewhat longer-drawn-out process requiring careful monitoring. Successful treatment involves adding the correct dose of a copper sulphate preparation – a point often overlooked in this connection is that this means water

conditioners should not be used during this period due to their copper-neutralizing effect. These two well-known fish diseases can crop up anywhere and at any time.

White spots, often known for short as ich, also spontaneously occur in fish whose immune systems have been weakened. Another hazard to some species of Lake Tanganyika cichlids, such as *Tropheus*, are intestinal parasites. These are caused in some cases by the fish themselves, and in others by incorrect feeding or stress. Under normal conditions the body remains in harmony with its natural bacterial population, but under conditions of stress or incorrect care the parasites may

gain the upper hand, and that is when your problems begin. This is why it is so important that your fish are kept under optimum conditions.

From personal experience I recommend adding salt, preferably sea salt, every time you change water. Use a heaped teaspoon to every 50 litres (11gal) of water. Treated this way, the fish visibly thrive, and salt, with its important trace elements, is the primary, simplest and most natural remedy for the rapid healing of external injuries, such as bite wounds, mild fungal infections, veil-like films over the eyes or damage in transit.

If your fish contract intestinal parasites despite this measure, perhaps because they were already ailing when you bought them, you will have to take action. Alongside general lack of appetite and apathy, affected fish will produce light-coloured, long faeces of a glassy appearance. The remedy of choice here is metronidazol, which is sold for human use under a variety of different names. Metronidazol is a prescription drug, so you will have to go to your vet to obtain it. Similar symptoms coupled with increasingly dark coloration and slimy white faeces are a sign of hexamite infection. Any unusual swelling of the belly can generally be combated by antibiotics regardless of its exact cause.

The following are necessary to ensure optimum conditions for your fish:

✓ regular water changes

✓ always thaw out frozen food before use

✓ avoid overfeeding

✓ take note of your fish's feeding habits (omnivore, herbivore, etc.) and provide suitably varied menus

✓ add extra vitamins regularly

✓ ensure correct stocking density for the size of your aquarium and the social behaviour of your fish

✓ avoid stress during transportation

✓ quarantine new stock in a separate tank

✓ continual observation

✓ prevention is better than cure

Before you place the first Lake Tanganyika cichlids into your aquarium, *Ancistrus* catfish or sucking loach will already have started their tireless work of devouring left-over food particles and algae. Fish other than cichlids occupying the aquarium must of course thrive under similar conditions and be behaviourally compatible with them. Interesting and often beautiful combinations result from adding a number of Lake Malawi mouthbrooders. Just imagine an aquarium populated with young *Tropheus duboisi* white-spotted cichlids, orangey-red *Pseudotropheus estherae* and luminescent light-blue *Pseudotropheus callainos* zebra cichlids. A breathtaking sight only matched by the fish of coral reefs. I would advise against stocking other species such as barbs or tetras since not only are their water and nutritional requirements very different, but also cichlids are too aggressive to mix with species of more peaceful dispositions. The following questions are decisive when deciding how to stock your tank:

How big is the aquarium?

How many fish of given species can be accommodated in a tank of this size, given their specific require-ments?

The final chapter, where a number of the more popular Lake Tanganyika cichlids are discussed, will offer you a small but representative selection to choose from. If you have difficulty choosing, your task can be simplified by opting for a standard introductory Lake Tanganyika selection. Regardless of your exact choice and of whether they come from a dealer or a breeder, you should carefully check the quality of the stock you acquire. By "quality" I mean the general physical condition of the fish. In this connection, you should avoid fish showing any of the following signs:

Hollow or sunken belly lines

Thin back region (so-called "knife-edge" back)

Eyes disproportionately large for body size

Any kind of injury or swelling

External parasites

Lack of appetite on introduction

Abnormal faeces

Sluggish swimming

Laboured respiration

Countless differently coloured regional variants of many species have now been identified, and these must be kept apart. There is also a danger of cross-breeding among closely related species, and this too must be avoided. Initially it is best always to purchase young farmed fish not less than 3cm (1.2in) in length. At first sight this may seem surprising given that wild-caught specimens of Lake Tanganyika cichlids are often available. However, these are understandably a

The captive-bred fish you buy should not be too small and should be in good condition. Neolampro-logus sp. "Daffodil".

Petrochromis species have a well-founded reputation for incompatibility and should only be kept in large groups in big tanks with a volume of 500 litres (110gal) or more.

good deal more expensive than farmed fish and generally also somewhat more difficult to handle. Properly looked after, your farmed cichlids will grow into excellent specimens which can often steal the show from many a wild-caught fish.

Another option which can be thoroughly recommended is to go for the widely available lake-bred farmed fish. In any case, be careful not to fall into financial ruin in your pursuit of Lake Tanganyika cichlids, which can

be heavy on the pocket: hold your enthusiasm in check. However, you should not hold back when it comes to the quantity purchased of any given species. In very few species is it easy to distinguish the two sexes, so that Lake Tanganyika cichlids must always be purchased "in bulk". A further reason for this is that you must expect some of your purchases to perish on statistical grounds alone, and it is important that your fish are offered a selection of sexual partners. Anyone purchasing a (presumed) breeding pair will lose out if one specimen dies, for finding and integrating a new partner is an extremely tricky business. More unscrupulous dealers often offer "pairs" of fish of species in which the sexes cannot be distinguished. Even experienced specialists may be unsure without a careful examination of the genital papillae.

A further point to note is that, in species where harem arrangements prevail, such as those of the *Cyprochromis* genus, there must be a preponderance of females. Other species, such as those of the *Tropheus* genus, show high levels of intraspecies aggression which can only be moderated by large numbers, to ensure that particular individuals do not bear the brunt of a dominant fish's aggression. As a rule of thumb, it is highly unlikely that you will be successful in the long term with less than five fish, and in a few cases, such as species of the genus *Petrochromis*, it is advisable to purchase at least ten individuals.

Now we finally come to the fish themselves. To commence I would like to introduce my own personal recommendation for a Lake Tanganyika dream team, suitable for an aquarium of dimensions 150cm x 50cm x 50cm (60in x 20in x 20in), with a volume of 375 litres (80gal):

The lower part of the tank would be adorned by lively upside-down catfish of the highly attractive *Synodontis multipunctatus* species (five specimens).

Meanwhile the upper region would be inhabited by energetic sardine cichlids of the *Cyprichromis leptosoma* species (three males and seven females).

Striped goby cichlids, *Eretmodus cyanostictus*, to peer out from the tufa rocks (one pair).

One pair of *Julidochromis dickfeldi* to glide among the many crevices overgrown with anubias.

To one side a pair of the yellow princess *Neolamprogus* sp. "Daffodil" energetically defend their patch.

However, the first thing to attract the observer's attention will be a hectic shoal of *Tropheus* cichlids of the *Tropheus* sp. "Cherry Spot" variety (three males and 12 females).

You would not believe what goes on! This is a fascinating mix, though constituting an entirely subjective selection which by no means overpopulates the tank. With a little luck you will observe young fry protecting their newly-hatched siblings,

Julidochromis
dickfeldi.

Tropheus *sp.*
"Cherry Spot".

Cyprichromis leptosoma spawning in open water, the goby cichlids transferring their brood from mouth to mouth, *Julidochromis* laying their green eggs in the porous rock and the quivering displays of *Tropheus* as the shoal establishes its "pecking order". And it would cap it all if you were to observe a cuckoo catfish inserting its own eggs among those of the nimble *Tropheus*, for this has hardly ever been observed. All in all, a show that fascinates me more than anything the TV companies have to offer!

While making no absolute guarantees about compatibility, I would like to recommend a few sample beginners' tanks of standard dimensions and stocked with some common Lake Tanganyika cichlids:

For a 45-litre (10gal) or 54-litre (12gal) aquarium
• One colony of *Neolamprologus multifasciatus* (ten specimens)

**45-litre
(50cm x 30cm x
30cm) or
54-litre
(60cm x 30cm x
30cm)**

37

Julidochromis
transcriptus
"Gombi".

Lamprologus
ocellatus.

**112-litre
(80cm x 35cm x
40cm)**

Telmatochromis will also squeeze itself into unoccupied snail shells. As usual, these species are very difficult to sex, and the number of specimens purchased has to be correspondingly high in order to ensure a high probability that your batch will contain at least one mating pair.

• or some *Lamprologus ocellatus* (five to eight specimens)
• or some *Julidochromis ornatus* (five to eight fry)
• or some *Julidochromis transcriptus* (five to eight fry)
• or some *Telmatochromis bifrenatus* (five to eight specimens).

The first two species must be provided with empty snail shells to hide in and for brooding. The two species of *Julidochromis* require a different form of concealment, which could, for example, take the form of slate tiles (red ones look good) or porous rock, while

For a 112-litre (25gal) aquarium
• One pair of *Neolamprologus brichardi* ("Daffodil" cichlids) and one pair of *Eretmodus cyanostictus* plus a few *Cyprichromis leptosoma* (three to five).

The well-known *Neolamprologus* cichlids patrol their territory imperiously, leading young of various sizes. The comical *Eretmodus* cichlids stick fairly close together and the male and female share the work of

mouthbrooding. The lively *Cyprichromis leptosoma* are ideal for populating the otherwise unused surface area of the tank.
- Or a few *Neolamprologus leleupi* (five to eight specimens)
plus some *Neolamprologus buescheri* (five to eight specimens)
and some "blue neon" *Paracyprichromis nigripinnis* (three to five specimens)

The luminescent yellow lemon cichlids and darker *Neolamprologus buescheri* make a very appealing

combination. Both species will pair off of their own accord. Once again the strikingly coloured sardine cichlids will populate the upper reaches of the aquarium tank elegantly.

For a 200-litre (44gal) or 250-litre (55gal) aquarium

With a tank 100cm (40in) wide, just 10cm (4in) more depth increases the volume by 50 litres (11gal). This also makes decorating the tank more straightforward.
- One group of *Tropheus duboisi* (ten fry)

Cyprichromis leptosoma "Kitumba".

200-litre (100cm x 40cm x 50cm) or 250-litre (100cm x 50cm x 50cm)

39

plus some *Neolamprologus cylindricus* (five to eight specimens) and some *Neolamprologus moorii* (five to eight fry) and a few *Spathodus erythrodon* (five to eight specimens)

A splendid combination, mixing mouthbrooders and cave spawners. You will be captivated by the fantastic markings of the young white-spotted cichlids, *Tropheus duboisi*, and watch fascinated as they develop their adult coloration. The transversely striped *Neolamprologus cylindricus* contrast excellently with the yellow-coloured young *Neolamprologus moorii* fish, which also undergo a colour transformation as they attain adulthood. The blue-flecked goby cichlids, *Spathodus erythrodon*, add life to the nooks and crannies of the lower third of the aquarium.

For a 240-litre (53gal) aquarium
• One group of *Tropheus* sp. "Bemba" (ten to 15 fry)
plus some *Julidochromis marlieri* (five to eight specimens)
and a pair of *Eretmodus cyanostictus*

The lively orange-striped *Tropheus* form the centrepiece of this aquarium. The strikingly patterned *Julidochromis marlieri* populate the nooks and crannies left free by the *Tropheus*, and *Eretmodus* are also very much at home here.
• or a few *Enantiopus melanogenys* (five to ten specimens)
plus some *Cyprichromis leptosoma* (five to ten specimens)

An excellent combination for connoisseurs of these special cichlids: sand cichlids and sardine cichlids in the same aquarium. However, sand cichlids are demanding fish and not really

240-litre (120cm x 40cm x 50cm)

Cyprichromis leptosoma.

Neolam-
prologus
buescheri.

Neolam-
prologus
cylindricus.

Paracypri-
chromis
nigripinnis
"Blue Neon".

Spathodus
erythrodon.

**For a 375-litre (82gal)
aquarium**
• A group of *Tropheus*
species (about 30
specimens)
• or a group of small
Petrochromis species
(about 20 specimens)
• or a group of *Simo-
chromis* species (about 20
specimens)
• or a group of *Opthal-
motilapia* species (10 to 15 specimens)
• or a group of *Cyphotilapia frontosa*
(about ten fry)

**375-litre
(150cm x 50cm x
50cm)**

suitable for beginners, who will find
Cyprichromis leptosoma easier to
handle. Their most important
requirement is a thin layer of sand in
which the territorially-minded males of
Enantiopus melanogenys can build
their nests.

These species aquariums can readily
be combined with various Tanganyika
cave spawners (for example *Julidochromis*) or Lake Malawi mouthbrooders

Tropheus *sp.*
"Orange Spot".

Enantiopus
melanogenys.

(for example *Pseudotropheus*).
However, the above-mentioned
mouthbrooders grow too large and
exhibit too much intraspecies aggression
to be kept in an aquarium that is less than
1.5 metres (5 ft) long.

As you will have seen, the available
variety and number of possible
combinations is so great that your
decision will be difficult, but certainly not
boring.

Before long you will develop a special
liking for particular varieties of Lake

Tanganyika cichlids. Do not be in too
much of a hurry, but remember:
resistance is futile!

Petrochromis
trewavasae.

Simochromis
pleurospilus.

Breeding Lake Tanganyika cichlids

Have you been paying attention? Then you now own the exclusive rights to a tiny slice of Africa's most ancient lake and its extraordinary inhabitants, the fascination of which will put much else into the shade. Be warned that once you have caught the Lake Tanganyika bug, you will never again be free of it.

Here are a few pieces of advice I would like to give you before you embark on your way:

Always try to simulate the natural environment of the lake and learn something about its various habitats. This will tell you everything you need to know about the conditions under which to keep your cichlids. Make sure you are aware of their special needs before you purchase them.

Learn the Latin Linnaean names of the species so that you will be able to describe them to others if necessary.

This is particularly important with Lake Tanganyika cichlids because the Latin names are frequently used, partly out of vanity, partly due to a lack of popular names.

You will also have to get used to the tongue-twisting names of the places where the fish originate and with which the fish are christened (so it sometimes seems) the moment three of them regularly visit the same spot.

Start out in a small way with a suitable tank, and do not spoil the ship for a ha'p'orth of tar, for example by trying to save money on the hardware.

Be patient when developing your aquarium and fish stocks.

Keep your eyes peeled for any unusual changes in the aquarium and in the fish population itself.

In the event of any disturbances of the aquarium ecosystem, always try to find out the root cause rather than just combating the symptoms.

Get advice from your local aquatic centre or pet shop.

Read up on the subject and, most important of all, regularly observe the activity in your aquarium.

Here, once again, is a summary of the most vital points to observe for successful aquarium keeping:

- ✓ Optimum water conditions
- ✓ Plenty of caves, nooks and crannies etc., for fish to hide in
- ✓ Harmonious fish population
- ✓ Correct nutrition
- ✓ Weekly water changes

Now prepare to enjoy many tranquil hours with your aquarium, and do not give up at the first sign of trouble.

After you have crossed the hurdle of successfully looking after your Lake Tanganyika cichlids, you can turn your thoughts to breeding them. It is entirely possible, of course, that your livestock will jump the gun and start breeding among themselves before you are ready for them, and often the first the aquarist knows about it is when fry can suddenly be seen flitting around in the tank. This is particularly common with the many cave spawners among Lake Tanganyika cichlids, since they lead a furtive life well out of the public eye. However, close observation will enable you to determine the territorial relationships and which specimens are pairing off with which other ones.

Sexual dimorphism among Lake Tanganyika cave spawners is particularly limited, making them difficult to sex. One good pointer, however, is their behaviour, as the males always have a strong impulse to occupy and defend a patch of territory. The only sure way is to examine the genital papillae with the help of a magnifying glass, and even this is not a straightforward business. In the females the genital opening is significantly bigger than in the males and also closer to the anus. In general, the males of many species are somewhat more solidly built and have more pointed fins. Since the fry in particular cannot be sexed, you should always buy at least four specimens in order to ensure a high probability of having a pair.

Fry and young fish can find hiding places from aggressors among the luxuriant vegetation.

Julidochromis
regani *"Kipili"*.

*A pair will
quickly form
from a shoal
of fry and
occupy their
own territory.*
Julidochromis
transcriptus
"Gombi".

Most cave spawners are mono-gamous, though this is not as obvious as with species that spawn in the open. Brood preparations cannot always be observed, but actual spawning is preceded by several preliminary dry runs. Fish which are ready to spawn are easy to spot due to their protruding genital papillae (known as spawning tubes). However, their mating efforts need a certain amount of practice, so do not be surprised if their first batch of eggs does not hatch out and the parents, for some incomprehensible reason, consume their own eggs. This may happen not once but several times. Be patient, however, because you will not have to wait long before breeding is successful. The fry hatch out of generally yellow-white eggs which are con-siderably larger than those of fish that spawn in open water. A relatively small number of fry, generally less than 100, hatch out after about three days. Many species spawn several times in quick succession and generally tolerate the fry within their own territories until they reach sexual maturity. If sexual maturity arrives early, this is far from meaning that you should notify your dealer about the impending arrival of offspring.

The best-known cave spawners are those of the *Lamprologus* genus and also the genera *Julidochromis*, *Telmatochromis* and *Chalinochromis*. If you are aiming to breed a particular species, you should set up a separate aquarium for these fish alone. The vegetation in this tank can be copious, because these species will not shred or dig up the greenery, and it provides a veritable jungle for them which can even be a life-saver for fish under attack. You should never place a single pair without any additional company in a tank, because they need a "whipping boy" on which to work off their aggression, and jointly defending a territory, and still more a brood, strengthens the relationship between any pair. If the male cannot dissipate his aggressive energy on these defensive duties, he will frequently turn on his mate, assuming threatening postures, taking on threatening coloration, etc. Additional fish in the aquarium, then, can act as a lightning conductor and ensure domestic harmony. However, note that the introduction of plecos will almost certainly not be conducive to breeding success since they may devour the spawn during the night.

Once an aquarium has been fully kitted out with fish, plants, rocks and substrate, you should do as little as possible and, beyond regular water changes, alter nothing. Many species are so sensitive that pairs will react to any disturbance by splitting up. The reason for this lies in the nature of their bond, which in many species comes from the territory they share rather than from the pair relationship in itself, so that the destruction of their hideout also leads to the destruction of the bond.

So much for the preliminaries. From this point on you can generally leave the fish to get on with it, for the majority of

Some cave spawners spawn several times in quick succession so that your aquarium will be populated by fry of varying size and age. Neolamprologus *sp.* "Daffodil".

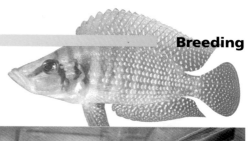

Lake Tanganyika cichlids are good parents who will raise their young on their own. Your job will be confined to providing special foods in generous quantities, and regularly changing the water, to ensure that the fry rapidly grow into healthy adult fish. If your cave spawners have produced young in a community aquarium, you will have to watch and hope that they are able to raise at least a few of their young. If this proves impossible due to population density in your aquarium, you can try transferring some of the fry to a separate tank. If you go about this in the right way, it should not cause distress. First you should prepare the nursery tank, establishing the correct water conditions, etc. Then use a length of thin tubing to suck some of the fry carefully out of the aquarium and into a bucket. However, never take all of the fry away from their parents. This will distress them and lead to disturbed behaviour such as eating of their own

A view of a turbulent and rather spartan-looking nursery aquarium for young fish.

49

spawn, behaviour which will probably persist in the long term.

If the fish persistently fail to rear any young, you can go one step further and incubate the eggs artificially. This can be done in a separate small, darkened tank to which a preparation to prevent fungal infection of the eggs has been added. The spawn must be transferred along with its substrate. The parents regularly fan the spawn to oxygenate it, and you must simulate this by gently aerating the eggs with an airstone placed where it will direct a stream of air past the spawn. Provided the eggs have been fertilized and you manage to prevent fungal infection, you will have a good chance of raising your own Lake Tanganyika cichlids.

Special features of mouthbrooders

Despite the fact that mouthbrooders have a completely different system of reproduction, it is possible to keep many cave spawners and mouthbrooders together in the same aquarium. The reproductive behaviour of mouthbrooders is more complex than that of cave spawners, and it involves many transitions and peculiarities, as you will find out right from the word go. Since many species of mouthbrooders are polygamous, you must ensure that there is a preponderance of females in the aquarium, a point to be borne in mind when purchasing your stock, though, as noted, sex differentiation is not easy. Too few females will lead to violent attacks. As with Lake Malawi cichlids, the males

are highly territorial and in most cases extremely aggressive, so plenty of other fish are needed to distract them and ensure no one individual bears the brunt of the attacks.

The courtship system is completely different: potent territorial males display

You must ensure that Cyphotilapia frontosa *receive adequate nutrition during rearing. Lively Lake Malawi cichlids are much quicker to find their food.*

in order to gain the favours of as many females as possible, spawning several times in succession with several different sexual partners. Receptive females only remain in intimate contact with the males during the brief period of mating. Thereafter they avoid all contact and look after their brood alone. Most mouthbrooders require a rock surface as a spawning substrate, while others will spawn on the floor of the tank. In contrast to cave spawners, you will often get the chance to observe mouth-brooders spawning due to the

51

Breeding

conspicuous nature of the males' displays. If you miss this little show. you will easily be able to identify mouth-brooding specimens due to the strong chewing motions they make. After 20 to 30 days the females release the fry, which are for obvious reasons relatively limited in number.

Once again a number of planned breeding options are open to you. The most natural course is to do nothing: if you have provided sufficient hiding places in which the fry can find relative safety from the attentions of the other aquarium inhabitants, you can simply sit

back and observe in the knowledge that a small select percentage will survive and eventually breed themselves. Each year, then, you will have to thin out the numbers in your tank in order both to prevent overpopulation and to stimulate the parents to breed again.

An alternative option is to transfer the mouthbrooding females into a separate spawning tank within the aquarium. These are commercially available in various sizes, primarily for live-bearing guppies/cyprinodonts. The mother will release the fry from her mouth after a two- to four-week brooding period.

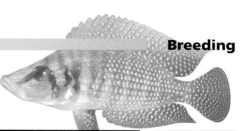

When the time comes to return the mother to the aquarium proper, you must seize the moment when all the fry have left their mother's mouth and move really quickly before they flee back into her protective throat sac.

A further option is to transfer the brooding fish to a separate aquarium, where she can pass the brooding period in a relaxed and stress-free environment.

It is possible to remove the fry forcibly from the mother's mouth by simply shaking them free, though this violent method should only be used as a last resort.

Artificial incubation of eggs is possible with mouthbrooders, but is doubly difficult since the chewing movements of the female must be imitated by artificial means. However, the fry themselves are large by comparison with cave spawners' fry, and rearing them once hatched is a straightforward matter. They should be fed on *Cyclops*, small brine shrimps and crushed dry food.

Enthusiasts have come up with a variety of ideas involving water jets for simulating the chewing movements of mouthbrooders in incubators for the artificial raising of their spawn.

It is better to separate mouthbrooding fish, for example in a home-made tank like this through which water can flow.

Selected species

In this chapter the best-known and most readily available Lake Tanganyika cichlids are briefly discussed in order to give you a representative idea of their variety and assist you in making your choices. Note, however, that this chapter does include species not recommended for beginners, but which belong in any representative list.

Altolamprologus compressiceps

Altolamprologus compressiceps is an interesting and highly striking Lake Tanganyika cichlid with a very high back and a deep mouth whose predatory purpose is soon revealed. In the lake they live in rocky habitats where their slender shape allows them to slip into narrow crevices in pursuit of prey. Their preferred victims are smaller fish and invertebrates. They should be treated with caution in aquariums since smaller inhabitants may fall victim to them. The aquarium itself should not be less than 80cm (30in) long, since male specimens can reach 15cm (6in) in length and are aggressive to one another. However, they do live in harmony with other aquarium occupants of equal size. The males are significantly bigger than the females, so that body length is generally a reliable indicator of gender.

Only a single pair should be placed in a mixed Lake Tanganyika aquarium. They require feeding with solid nourishment such as frozen shrimps and the like. *Altolamprologus compressiceps* prefer narrow crevices as a spawning ground, and empty sea snail shells have been successfully used to breed them in captivity. The female will squeeze inside and lay up to 300 eggs. After fertilizing them, the male plays little further role in rearing the brood, limiting himself to defending the territory. Since the female looks after the brood virtually alone in

Altolampro-
logus
compressiceps.

the wild too, you should provide caves or shells into which only the smaller female can squeeze since the male is extremely aggressive and will harass the female, so that she will need a secure place of refuge for herself and also, during brooding, for her offspring. *Altolamprologus compressiceps* fry, like those of the very similar *Altolamprologus calvus*, are renowned for their slow growth, even when given the best of care. They are widely available at aquatic centres in a variety of different naturally-occuring colorations.

Callochromis macrops

The two large eyes of these well-known sand cichlids are a particularly striking feature. Another peculiarity of the species is that, unusually among Lake Tanganyika cichlids, the males and females are clearly distinct. The males grow to about 12cm (5in) in length and have a reddish coloration, whereas the females are silver in colour. The males also have a marking on their anal fins of variable clarity which serves to attract the female's attention during mating.

In Lake Tanganyika the species chiefly inhabits shallow waters over a sandy bed, which it sifts through in the search for invertebrates. Accordingly the substrate in their aquarium should also be sand. In the aquarium *Callochromis macrops* will accept any food in replacement for their natural

Above:
Altolampro-
logus
compressiceps
"Golden Head".

*Left: Shell-
dwelling*
compressiceps.

Callochromis
macrops *"Red"*:

55

Chalino-
chromis *sp.*
"Bifrenatus".

diet. The level of intraspecies aggression is very high, particularly among territorial males, so it is advisable to keep a small group of them, and to minimize the problem further the tank should be at least 120cm (48in) long. *Callochromis macrops* do not form bonds between mating pairs. The courting male entices the female to a prepared hollow where spawning takes place, and the female then broods alone for a period of about three weeks.

The best tank companions for *Callochromis macrops* are featherfins and other sand cichlid species. It comes in several regional variants, the best-known of which remains the "Red Macrops", which can be exquisitely coloured.

Chalinochromis brichardi

The elongated *Chalinochromis* with its striking head markings and the dark spot on its dorsal fin lives in Lake Tanganyika in pairs on rocky shorelines, lurking among the many crevices where they feed chiefly on tiny snails. Although the fish can reach a length of almost 15cm (6in) in the wild, they normally remain

much smaller than this in the aquarium, and are strongly reminiscent of the slender cichlids of the *Julidochromis* genus in behaviour as well as in appearance. Unfortunately, this resemblance is more than skin-deep, and undesired cross-breeding can occur in captivity. The adult male can be distinguished by the slight bulge on its forehead. If this bulge is clearly apparent, then you only need to buy one pair, otherwise you should purchase at least five fishes in order to ensure a good probability that you have specimens of both sexes. Their aquarium should be at least 60cm (24in) long. They are happy in mixed company, but being typical cave spawners, they do need plenty of hiding places.

Cyclops and dried foods are best for them, and larger food such as frozen shrimps should be avoided since they have difficulty swallowing and digesting them. If the hiding places you have provided do not suit the fish as spawning grounds, you can add various different kinds of cave to the tank.

Pairs look after their brood together and guard their territory energetically. Fry, which grow to maturity in their parents' territory, should be feed with *Artemia* nauplii.

Various different species are available commercially, among them the *Chalinochromis* sp. "Bifrenatus", "Ndobhoi" and "Popelini". Details of their care and breeding are similar to those for the *Telmatochromis* genus, whose most common species,

Telmatochromis bifrenatus, is most often seen.

Cyphotilapia frontosa
Frontosa cichlid

These are predatory fish of striking appearance which live in the deeper reaches of the rocky coastal waters, growing to over 30cm (12in) in length. In adulthood the males become markedly different in appearance from the females, developing a pronounced bulge on their foreheads, as well as becoming much larger and growing much longer fins. Both sexes share similarly attractive coloration, however. Despite their size they are a peaceable species showing little urge to defend a territory. This tendency is so marked that adult males even allow themselves to be driven off by smaller but more aggressive species. Because of this, care must be taken that young fish are not too seriously harassed in mixed-species aquariums, and unfortunately lively, energetic Lake Tanganyika or Lake Malawi cichlid species are not suitable tank companions.

You should observe carefully whether the fish are receiving adequate nutrition. *Cyphotilapia frontosa* grow very slowly and eat little. Despite their size they do not need excessively large aquariums – tanks 120cm (48in) in length will suffice. Although swimming space is more important to these fishes than hiding places, you should nevertheless provide caves for concealment purposes. If you purchase larger specimens, you should

ensure there is a preponderance of females, since this is a typical mouthbrooder in which the females brood alone. They prefer to spawn on the aquarium substrate. Even when courting and mating the fish do not become particularly lively, and as a result spawning is seldom observed. The fish appear to become more active at night. As discussed above, brooding females can be transferred to a separate aquarium, where they will release an average of 50 fry or so after about four weeks.

A range of different colour variants are

Cyphotilapia frontosa "Blue Zaire".

now available at widely differing prices. Most of these are farmed fish, wild fish being the highly-priced preserve of specialist collectors due to the difficulty involved in catching them. Perhaps the most attractive, and easily the most expensive morph of *Cyphotilapia frontosa* is the "Blue Zaire".

Cyphotilapia
frontosa.

Cyprichromis leptosoma

Cyprichromis leptosoma live in large shoals in the open waters of Lake Tanganyika, where these untypically-shaped cichlids feed off animal plankton which they suck in through their extensible mouths. The sexes are easy to distinguish, the males being multicoloured, the females plain blue. There are several different regional colour variants of the male. Both sexes grow to about 10cm (4in) in length. *Cyprichromis leptosoma* are typical mouthbrooders where the lively males compete for the favours of many females and no bonds form between the sexes. However, they do have one almost unique trait, which is that the fish simply spawn in open water without recourse

to any form of substrate. Their polygamous lifestyle means that there must be a preponderance of females in the aquarium. The fry cannot be sexed since the distinctive male coloration does not start to manifest itself until they reach about 5cm (2in) in length. The energetic males are only moderately aggressive by the standards of Lake Tanganyika cichlids, and several can be kept without difficulty in tanks measuring 80cm (30in) or longer. However, one difficulty in keeping them is their tendency to spring out of the water, making a hood essential.

Cyprichromis leptosoma are highly susceptible to damage during capture, transportation and the settling-in period, and care must be taken

Cyprichromis
leptosoma
"Kitumba".

Cyprichromis
leptosoma
"Chipimbi".

gradually to reduce any disparity in water quality before introducing them to the aquarium. If they feel unwell they retract all their fins, and should this happen a little salt and a few vitamins will help. They are highly sensitive to lack of oxygen and will be the first to react should levels in the tank fall. They cannot withstand temperatures above 30°C (86°F), and must be fed on small shrimps, deep frozen *Cyclops* and live *Artemia* being ideal. *Cyprichromis* are the only one of my Lake Tanganyika cichlids that I feed on small organisms that I catch myself. They can be bred either in separate tanks in which floating plants providing cover, or by isolating mouthbrooding females within the community aquarium. They should only share a tank with peacable, less aggressive species. Several different regional variants of *Cyprichromis leptosoma* are available commercially, for example the "Blue Flash", "Malasa", "Mupulungu" and "Kitumba" varieties.

Enantiopus melanogenys
Enantiopus melanogenys is the best-known and possibly the most attractive

59

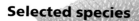

Xenotilapia
flavipinnis.

Enantiopus
melanogenys.

there should be a preponderance of females, though achieving this is not straightforward since the species is very difficult to sex. However, if you only keep a single male with many females, it will rarely display its striking courtship coloration: competition is healthy. Once again the females undertake brooding duties unaided, and in the aquarium they may be isolated when due to release their fry. Fish of the previously discussed species *Cyprichromis leptosoma* provide ideal aquarium companions for *Enantiopus melanogenys*.

If you plan to specialize in this kind of species, you should really keep them alone in their own aquarium, otherwise they will never truly thrive. Sand cichlids are very timid, tend to leap out of the water and are highly susceptible to harm, and as such are not suitable for beginners.

Apart from *Enantiopus melanogenys*, the similar-looking and -behaving species *Xenotilapia ochrogenys* and *Xenotilapia sima* are commercially available from time to time, while two other *Xenotilapia* species with totally different behaviour patterns (the eggs are switched from one parent to the other midway through the mouth-brooding period), *Xenotilapia papilio* and *Xenotilapia flavipinnis*, are highly popular among specialists.

of the so-called sand cichlids, and belongs in any representative list. The males display impressive coloration during courtship. In Lake Tanganyika they occupy areas of sandy coastline, where large colonies of territorial males build sand nests and then perform courtship displays to any passing silvery-yellow female. The species, which grows to about 15cm (6in) in length, feeds by continually sieving through the sand for edible items, then expelling the sand and debris through openings behind the gill flaps. Accordingly, a sand cichlid aquarium must have a fine substrate and be at least one metre (40in) long. Ideally,

Eretmodus cyanostictus
Striped goby cichlid

The jerky, stop-start mode of locomotion of all four species of goby cichlid is reminiscent of the somewhat comical movement of the well-known *Eretmodus* genus. The behaviour of the fish, which often peer inquisitively out from crevices, is quite distinctive and amusing to watch. In Lake Tanganyika the fish, which grow to about 10cm (4in) in length, live in pairs in extremely shallow waters where they feed by scraping vegetation off rocks. The two sexes are very hard to distinguish, though when fully grown the males are generally somewhat more robustly built and have a slight forehead bulge.

Eretmodus cyanostictus are ideal candidates for a community aquarium, where they will lurk in concealed locations.

Unusually among mouthbrooders they form monogamous bonds, a characteristic strengthened by the fact that the pairs share the task of mouthbrooding, with the females transferring the fry to the male after about 12 days. Because of this, in planned breeding programmes the male should be added to the breeding tank after a further five days. Beforehand you must ensure that the fish are well nourished with suitable plant materials. *Eretmodus cyano- stictus* are another species highly

Eretmodus cyanostictus.

61

sensitive to low oxygen levels, and require the regular addition of fresh water. Wild-caught fish of the "Burundi" variety of *Eretmodus cyanostictus* are often commercially available. Somewhat more colourful are the blue-spotted variant from Zambia, the dark one from Tanzania and the orange coloured variety from Kigoma.

can reach 15cm (6in) in length, and in Lake Tanganyika they inhabit rocky stretches of coastline where they feed, among other things, on small snails. The best aquarium food for them are *Cyclops* and *Daphnia*. With their tiny, pointed mouths, the fry can only consume very small particles of food.

It is impossible to distinguish the

Julidochromis marlieri.

Julidochromis marlieri
Plaid Julie, Marlier's Julie

Julidochromis marlieri is the best-known member of the highly popular *Julidochromis* genus, of which five species are currently recognized. These long, slender, splendidly marked cichlids

males and females from their external appearance, and it is only when courting and spawning occur that one can tell which individuals belong together and what gender they are. The fish then form monogamous pairs which look after their young together. Once a

harmonious pair has formed, the fish will spawn several times in quick succession. Some *Julidochromis marlieri* lay a number of greenish eggs almost every week. The species can readily be kept in a mixed-species Lake Tanganyika aquarium, but they will require plenty of rockwork in which to hide. The cave spawners among them favour slate, porous rock and a varied selection of caves in which to establish their territories and choose their spawning ground, which they then defend vigorously. The fish also show marked intraspecies aggression. Local races of this species too have now been identified, but commercially available specimens are generally farmed, and not always from the most handsomely marked parent fish.

Neolamprologus brevis
Brevis shell dweller

Perhaps the best-known of the shell-dwelling cichlids, this species lives in silty areas of the Lake Tanganyika coastline in the vicinity of empty snail shells, which they generally bury in the substrate so that only the openings to them remain visible. They grow to just 5cm (2in) in length – the usual diminutive size for a shell-dwelling cichlid – and show marked sexual dimorphism, with the males being more heavily built, considerably larger and more intensely coloured than the females. The smaller females are always the first to enter their shell home, and the species form the pair bonds typical of cave spawners, with the females doing the brooding while the males guard their territories. Uniquely among Lake Tanganyika shell-dwelling cichlids, male and female partners alike use the same shell both as a hiding place and brooding ground. Aquarists should not keep more than one pair of this highly territorial species and should provide them with a sandy substrate as they are keen burrowers. Tanks of 40 litres (9gal) or more are sufficient to keep a single pair.

Empty garden snail shells may be used in place of those of Lake Tanganyika species, and a selection of several of

Neolampro-logus brevis.

these should be made available. Without shells fish of this species are effectively homeless. Crustacea such as *Cyclops*, waterfleas and *Artemia* are all suitable food. The fish are difficult to extract from the tank since they always flee into their shells at the first sign of trouble. The spawn or fry, though, can readily be

63

Neolamprologus meeli.

transferred to a separate aquarium by simply lifting out the shell they are housed in. However, they are generally easy to breed in community aquariums, though care must be taken to ensure the fry receive the right nutrition. If necessary you can feed them directly using a pipette. Apart from *Neolamprologus brevis*, a variety of other shell-dwelling cichlids are available, all requiring similar care though the behaviour of each species is slightly different. Examples include *Neolamprologus multifasciatus*, *N. meeli* and *Lamprologus ocellatus*.

Neolamprologus signatus.

Neolamprologus brichardi
Fairy cichlid

The so-called fairy cichlid or lyretail lamprologus is one of the most popular of all Lake Tanganyika cichlids, and is widely available at aquatic centres. However, their elegant swimming style and graceful appearance are highly deceptive, for these well-known fish are extremely tough characters and anything but shrinking violets. In Lake Tanganyika these c.10cm-(4in-) long fish live in large shoals of several hundred fishes, which swarm around above their hiding places in search of food in the form of animal plankton. *Neolamprologus brichardi* is a typical cave spawner forming a monogamous pair. The sexes are very difficult to

Neolamprologus similis.

Neolampro-
logus pulcher.

Neolampro-
logus brichardi.

tell apart, though adult males are generally some-what more power-fully built and have longer fin tips. If several fry are introduced into an aquarium, a pair will quickly em-erge and stake out a territory to defend. It is very important to provide them with plenty of hiding places, and the aquarium furnishings you use to this end are limited only by your imagination. This species is highly aggressive towards other fish and its sharp teeth can cause serious injury.

Neolamprologus brichardi have extraordinary reproductive behaviour. They spawn several times in quick succession, and older offspring aid their parents in looking after the brood, protecting their smaller siblings by assisting in the defence of the parental territory – behaviour unique among fish. The parents themselves do not have an especially strong bond and do not care intensively for the brood – it is only the territory itself that is defended vigorously. Thus it is not difficult to breed the species successfully in a mixed-species aquarium. Apart from the best-known species *Neolamprologus brichardi*, other commonly available species include the handsome *Neolamprologus* sp. "Daffodil", *N.* sp.

"Walteri" and the red-spotted *Neolamprologus pulcher*.

Neolamprologus leleupi
Lemon cichlid
The very well-known lemon cichlids live solitary lives in Lake Tanganyika's rocky biotope and feed on small crustacea. The species show little sexual dimorphism, and both sexes grow to about 10cm (4in) in length. Adult males are slightly more powerfully built and may develop a slight forehead bulge. They are typical cave spawners and only

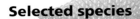

Neolampro-
logus leleupi.

Neolampro-
logus
cylindricus.

This striking cichlid makes an interesting addition to mixed-species Lake Tanganyika tanks, and like all Lake Tanganyika cichlids, and most markedly the cave spawners, it requires plenty of hiding places.

To ensure that it retains its luminous yellow colour in the aquarium it must be fed on *Cyclops*, *Daphnia* and *Artemia* supplemented by coloured flake food. A few flowerpots or ceramic caves provide ideal brood places. As usual with cave spawners, the female is solely responsible for looking after the brood of young.

In small tanks it is possible that the male will harass the female so severely come together in the wild for reproductive purposes. In aquariums, lemon cichlids are territorial and aggressive towards their own species. For this reason only one pair should be kept per aquarium, and superfluous specimens should be removed from the tank once a pair appear ready for mating.

that he has to be removed, in which case he can be returned to the tank once the female's swollen belly shows that she is about to spawn.

Several different morphs of *Neolamprologus leleupi* have been distinguished, some of which can even be surprisingly dark in colour. The popular and recently-discovered species *Neolamprologus buescheri* and *Neolamprologus cylindricus* have behaviour patterns that are similar to those of the lemon cichlid.

Neolamprologus tretocephalus.

Neolamprologus tretocephalus *juvenile.*

Neolamprolgus tretocephalus
The strikingly marked *Neolamprologus tretocephalus* lives in pairs in rocky and sandy areas of Lake Tanganyika, where

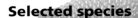

Neolampro-
logus moorii,
juvenile.

Neolampro-
logus moorii,
adult.

territorial pairs hunt for hidden invertebrates, chiefly snails, which they crush with their powerful pharyngeal bones. Once again males and females are hard to distinguish. In the wild they can grow to 15cm (6cm) in length, but in an aquarium they generally remain significantly smaller. At first sight they are readily confused with the species *Neolamprologus sexfasciatus* and *Cyphotilapia frontosa. Neolamprologus tretocephalus* shows a high degree of intraspecies aggression and should be kept in pairs in spacious mixed-species tanks well over 100 litres (22gal) in volume. The pair will sometimes drive away any superfluous members of their species themselves. Flowerpots or ceramic caves make acceptable hiding or brooding places. The aquarium must

Ophthalmo-
tilapia
ventralis.

have plenty of hiding places in which harassed fish can conceal themselves, and even the female member of a pair is sometimes not safe from her mate. Once again, the presence of other species helps to divert some of this aggression. The female can lay several hundred eggs in the cave, which is defended from intruders by the male.

They are easy to feed, readily accepting solid replacement food. This is another species with a tendency to leap out of the water. *Neolamprologus tretocephalus* is a highly attractive and typical cave spawner and is fascinating to observe. Similarly aggressive are the now-scarce *Neolamprologus tetra-canthus* and the ever-popular *Neolamprologus moorii* with their distinctive colouring.

Ophthalmotilapia ventralis

The best-known member of this genus of striking fish, the males of which sport extended ventral fins, is *Ophthal-motilapia ventralis*. Like the sand cichlids, *Ophthalmotilapia* live in mixed sand and rock areas of Lake Tanganyika, where the 15cm- (6in-) long males burrow out spawning hollows next to each other and then perform courtship displays to passing females. In the right light the males show up as an exquisite luminiscent blue, whereas the females are a much more inconspicuous silvery colour. Unfortunately the males develop their adult coloration very late, meaning it is impossible to distinguish the sex of young fish. When the males feel under pressure or unwell, they take on the same coloration as females and young

69

Selected species

Ophthalmo-
tilapia nasuta.

Aulonocranus
dewindti.

fish. The species is a typical mouth-brooder in which the males are only interested in passing on their genes to as many females as possible, while the females, which brood alone, are only interested in selecting the most handsome, qualitatively best, sexual partner.

During the impressive courtship display and mating the full glory of the male's coloration will impress any onlooker. These specimens need plenty of space in the aquarium, which must be at least 1.5 metres (60in) long. The aquarium substrate material must be as fine as possible. If there are several males, individuals who are ready to mate will soon start building their hollows and competing for the favour of the females. It is advisable to transfer brooding females to a separate aquarium where they can release their young in a stress-free environment.

Aggressive species, such as other Lake Malawi or Lake Tanganyika cichlid mouthbrooders, are highly unsuitable as aquarium sharers, as *Ophthalmotilapia ventralis* will completely fail to thrive in their presence. Lake Tanganyika cave spawners are far more suitable companions, but fans of *Ophthalmotilapia ventralis* will in any case prefer to breed them in a separate, spacious aquarium. Several regional races of *Ophthalmotilapia ventralis* have now been identified, many of them exquisitely coloured. Related *Ophthalmotilapia* species requiring similar treatment are *O. boops*, *nasuta*, *heterodonta*, and also the superb-looking *Cyathopharynx furcifer*, which can fetch fancy prices.

Paracyprichromis nigripinnis
Blue neon
At the end of the 1980s a strikingly coloured new cichlid species was discovered which, for obvious reasons, soon became known as the "Blue Neon". This species belongs to that untypical group of cichlids known to aquarists as sardine cichlids. In contrast to evenly coloured species such as *Cyprichromis leptosoma*, the males of the species are distinguished by stippled blue lines which run the length of their bodies. In the aquarium it soon becomes clear that this *Cyprichromis* species behaves very differently from its cousins, which in itself justifies classifying it as belonging to a different genus. *Paracyprichromis nigripinnis*, the species of which the blue neon is a variant, is far less temperamental than related species such as *Cyprichromis leptosoma*. The species is closely tied to its substrate, even sometimes spawning on sheer rockfaces, whereas *Cyprichromis leptosoma* always spawns in open water.

The fish must be fed on fresh crustacea, preferably live ones. Hand-reared brine shrimps are ideal, and freshly caught *Cyclops* and *Daphnia* are also suitable. They use their protruding mouths to suck in or pick up their food. The right aquarium companions are as important to them as correct nutrition, and the larger, more aggressive Lake Tanganyika cichlids are not suitable company, particularly for the blue neon, which is less robust and significantly smaller than *Cyprichromis leptosoma*. They also require regular water changes if they are to thrive, at least half the aquarium contents every week. As noted previously, *Cyprichromis leptosoma* are poor travellers and easily stressed. *Paracyprichromis nigripinnis* and the related species *P. brieni* generally seem to be somewhat more sensitive and susceptible to illness than their *Cyprichromis* cousins.

71

The picture shows a mating pair of the exquisitely marked Para-cyprichromis nigripinnis *"Blue Neon".*

Tropheus duboisi
White-spotted cichlid

The well-known white-spotted cichlid is one of the most popular of all Lake Tanganyika cichlids, and is familiar to almost all aquarists with its distinctive polka-dot markings. The coloration of the young fish, which is reminiscent of

less than ten, and they are positively enormous in comparison to those of many other species. Naturally the fish cannot brood many of these pea-sized eggs in their mouths, and after four weeks they release very large (more than 1cm/0.4in long) and robust fry to the safety of the rocks. In aquariums the species is very territorial and shows a high level of intraspecies aggression, and it is advisable to keep at least ten specimens in an aquarium at least 120cm (48in) in length.

Males and females cannot be distinguished except by examining the genital papillae. Nutrition is a critical matter for this herbivorous species, which very readily suffer from often fatal intestinal disorders. They should be fed on *Cyclops*, *Daphnia*, small quantities of *Mysis* shrimp and *Artemia* plus plant flakes containing plenty of *Spirulina*. Do not feed them on live food or mosquito larvae, even frozen ones. Any frozen food must be fully thawed out before being fed to them.

many coral reef species, will fascinate every observer. However, these cichlids undergo a striking colour change in later life, sadly losing their splendid markings after about a year, though their adult coloration can also be very pleasing. Members of this species live solitary lives in the lake, feeding on rock vegetation.

Males and females only ever associate for purposes of mating, displaying typical mouthbrooder reproductive behaviour, with the females brooding alone. The female spawns very few eggs, normally

The females must be provided with décor or rockwork including plenty of hiding places in which they can release their fry in relative safety. In community tanks there is a good chance that the majority of the fry will survive. Alternatively, the female can be

transferred to a separate tank. However, care must be taken since the species forms closed societies within the aquarium which will reject any newcomer, or even sick members of their own community, and after just two weeks' isolation some females will be treated as newcomers, sometimes even being hounded to their deaths. *Tropheus duboisi* are compatible with other mouthbrooding Lake Malawi and Lake Tanganyika herbivores. Cave spawners will also find sufficient sanctuary in their company, since *Tropheus duboisi* are not aggressive towards other species. A popular and closely related species are the various forms of *Tropheus moorii*, which thrives under very similar conditions and mixes very well with *Tropheus duboisi*.

Tropheus moorii

Tropheus moorii count among cichlid fans' all-time favourites. This is no surprise: although these fish are not easy to keep, they exercise a magical fascination over Lake Tanganyika cichlid enthusiasts. For one thing there is the exquisite appearance of many morphs, and on top of that there is their lively and captivating behaviour, which glues many an enthusiast to the aquarium.

Tropheus moorii can be the occasion of great sadness as well as great pleasure, a characteristic they combine in a very noteworthy way. This contradiction means they provoke a unique passion among their fans such as I have never observed in any other type of fish. To this you can add the rareness of some variants and the high prices they can

A *Tropheus duboisi* which has almost completely lost its juvenile markings.

Tropheus sp. "*Kachese Red*".

fetch, giving them an unwitting role as status symbols among aquarists. But believe me, *Tropheus* cichlids are worth both the money and the trouble!

Until a few years ago, any *Tropheus* that did not look like *Tropheus duboisi* was described as one of these. Strictly speaking, however, this name only applies to the now scarce, but for many years predominant, yellowy-red Rutunga form. Furthermore, it is also not strictly correct to classify all variants of the species as *Tropheus moorii*. However, this is not of great interest to us here.

The more you know about the *Tropheus* genus, the more fascinating it becomes, and the thrill of novelty is

Tropheus *sp.* *"Lupota"*.

always very much to the foreground, as new variants that you "just have to have" turn up continually. In recent years some superb morphs which are among the most striking of all aquarium fish have been exported, and some aquarists have teetered on the brink of financial ruin in their efforts to acquire specimens of every new variant. However, for many the disappointment is great as they experience their first losses for, like *Tropheus duboisi* and all other *Tropheus* species, *Tropheus moorii* are highly susceptible to intestinal disorders which can often have a fatal outcome. If you give up on the genus in frustration, though, you are likely to suffer a relapse,

as all other fish are prone to seem boring after you have kept the hectic and energetic *Tropheus*. Perhaps you too will fall for the peculiar charms of these cichlids as you progress to become an advanced Lake Tanganyika aquarist. Be warned though that it is a lifelong sentence!

A closing word

With the assistance of this little guide you should not go too far wrong, so I'll leave you alone with your Lake Tanganyika cichlids now, in the hope that I have been able to furnish simple answers to your most pressing questions.

And now it's up to you!

For further information
about the full Interpet range of
aquatic and pet titles, please
write to:
Interpet Publishing,
Vincent Lane,
Dorking,
Surrey,
RH4 3YX